LOCKDOWN

A full-length dramedy by
Julia Edwards

Commissioned by South Coast Repertory

www.youthplays.com
info@youthplays.com
424-703-5315

CAST OF CHARACTERS

F ALICE, the quiet girl who reads the dictionary.

F DARCY, senior class president, rule hound. — *Derek ? M*

M GARRETT, friendly surfer dude.

M JEREMY, computer guru/ black market ringleader.

F KATARINA, substitute teacher, loses it.

F LEEANN, princess (chain-smoking, compulsive lying variety).

F LEX, another righteous feminist bound for Smith College.

F LILY, a.k.a., Crazy Lily, can hear Satan (or so she says).

F MIA, theatre spaz.

F MORGAN, retro chick.

F PIGEON, painfully shy, frog advocate.

F ROSIE, tough girl from Brooklyn, hates California.

F SIMONE, wears black, digs Nietzsche. — *Simon ? - M*

M SQUID, anti-authority skater punk.

M VINCE, Jeremy's "bodyguard" and role-playing junkie.

PLACE

The "CliffsNotes *[5 punk]* Library: More Books, Less Filling"—a new corporate vision of the school library complete with hidden cameras; corporate banners (The Three R's: Reading, 'Riting, and Reese's Pieces; School is Kool... Kool does not condone smoking for children under 18); dorky posters (David Hasselhoff Digs Reading, a computer generated 3-D poster of a Big Mac); and so many computers these kids have just got to learn something.

TIME

Soon?

SCENE 1

(A SCHOOL BELL rings. The library clock reads 1:20 PM. Several students are already present. ALICE, hands over her ears, reads the dictionary. SIMONE, the nihilist chick in black, listens to her CD player and reads Sartre's No Exit. LEX, a righteous feminist bound for Smith College, devours the latest Ms. Magazine. MIA, an eccentrically dressed theatre spaz, practices a monologue to herself. A line has formed at the library monitor's desk: first in line is LEEANN, the bad girl princess who chatters on her cell phone.)

LEEANN: That is SO not fair—she is such a cow!... Oh my God! That is SO gross!... OK, I'll be there at 7. Kiss, kiss!

(Leeann hangs up and makes another call. Second in line is ROSIE, a recent (and unwilling) transplant from her native Brooklyn. She waits impatiently. JEREMY, the library monitor/ black market ringleader, enters with VINCE, the somewhat disheveled role-playing junky and his right hand man. They set up at the monitor station.)

VINCE: So Josh says he wants to kill these hyenas who weren't evil or magical or anything and the Dungeon Master is like: Dude, they're just hyenas.

JEREMY: Vince. Tuck your shirt in.

(Vince tucks his shirt in.)

VINCE: But Josh just starts wailing on them with his Plus-2 Mace. Isn't that messed up?

JEREMY: Yeah. Start loading up the cart. We've got to get through Q by the end of the period.

VINCE: Check.

(Vince obeys his order. Jeremy starts tapping away at his computer.)

JEREMY: *(To Leeann:)* What can I do you for, Princess?

LEEANN: *(Into phone:)* Kiss, kiss! Gotta go! *(Femme fatale-ish:)* I don't normally do this.

JEREMY: That's what they all say.

LEEANN: It's just that my boyfriend, you know, he's an agent, you know, in Hollywood. He handles...big people. I mean...Tom Cruise big, OK? I can't really tell you who he handles, but—

JEREMY: They're big. Got it. Time's money and money's time so let's cut to the chase.

LEEANN: American History mid-term.

JEREMY: Teacher?

LEEANN: Snook.

JEREMY: Ooh... That's not going to be easy. He keeps his tests locked up pretty tight.

LEEANN: Can you do it or not?

JEREMY: We put a man on the moon; of course I can do it. But it'll cost ya.

LEEANN: How much?

(Jeremy gives Vince the signal. Vince whispers an amount in her ear; she's aghast.)

Do you take credit cards?

JEREMY: But of course.

(She hands over a credit card. GARRETT, the friendly surfer dude, ambles into the library.)

GARRETT: So this is what the library looks like. Oo. *(Acting all quiet:)* Sorry, studious people. You must be the Library Monitor Man.

(He hands over a pass.)

JEREMY: What are you in for?

GARRETT: Yeah, I don't know, Mrs. Plant thinks I've got a tardy problem and she's run out of other punishments.

JEREMY: Stamp him.

(Vince stamps the pass.)

GARRETT: *Sports Illustrated?*

(Vince points.)

You're a good man. Whoa — Leeann!

LEEANN: Garrett.

GARRETT: Who's your friend?

LEEANN: Never seen her before.

GARRETT: Tell her I think I'm in love with her.

ROSIE: Get bent, weirdo.

GARRETT: No, tell her I'm *definitely* in love with her.

LEX: Can you keep it down? Some people are trying to do this thing called "read."

GARRETT: Lex — my Favorite Feminist. You better not be hogging the Swimsuit Issue.

LEX: Believe it or not, I actually read things where women get to keep their clothes on and maintain this thing called self-respect. You should try it.

(Garrett picks up the coveted Sports Illustrated.)

GARRETT: *(Drooling:)* Oh, yes...

(Garrett plops down next to Lex, puts his feet up, and starts to "read.")

I'm sorry. What was that you said?

LEX: Seventy-two more days until college. Just seventy-two more days until college.

(DARCY, the senior class president, marches in with her loyal servants: MORGAN, a Retro Chick complete with poodle skirt and every Sanrio accessory that's made it through customs; and PIGEON, a painfully shy animal-lover, who juggles an armful of posters. Darcy approaches Jeremy with passes outstretched.)

DARCY: Official Class President business.

MORGAN: We're here to hang posters for the prom.

DARCY: At Principal Walters' request. Note the signature at the bottom.

(Pigeon loses control of the posters and they all end up on the ground.)

PIGEON: Uh oh.

DARCY: For crying out loud, Pigeon.

PIGEON: I'm sorry. It was the frogs. I usually smuggle them out one at a time but tomorrow's dissection day so I had to grab them all at once and they're getting a little rowdy. *(To frogs:)* It's OK, guys, we'll be home soon. You want an olive?

DARCY: I don't know why I bother sometimes.

MORGAN: Because you care.

DARCY: I know. It really takes it out of me sometimes. It really does. But—I guess that's what being a public servant is all about.

(Jeremy hands back the passes.)

Come on, ~~girls~~. Let's poster.

(Darcy directs Morgan and Pigeon to hang perky prom posters. A second SCHOOL BELL rings. LILY, the punk chick who comes from money but pretends she doesn't, slams into the library just as the bell stops ringing. Lily walks past Leeann and Rosie and hands her pass to Jeremy.)

LILY: Here.

LEEANN: Hey, Lily.

(Leeann taps Lily on the shoulder.)

Hey. Lily.

(Lily slowly turns around.)

There's a line, in case you didn't notice.

LILY: Eat glass, Leeann. Besides, I'm just getting my pass signed. I don't need someone to steal test answers for me. *(To Jeremy:)* Hey, can I have that sometime this year?

JEREMY: I can't make out the teacher's name. Who signed this?

(Lily gets in Jeremy's face.)

LILY: It was that dorky history teacher with the blue cardigan and the comb-over — I don't know what his friggin name is — Moss or Jenson or something like that. What am I — school personnel? Now, what do you say you stamp my pass, like a good Library Monitor, and let me do my homework?

(Jeremy knows something's up — but would rather not get into it with Lily.)

JEREMY: *(To Vince:)* Stamp her.

(Vince stamps the pass. Lily grabs it and plops down in a corner and doodles Satan worship symbols on her arms.)

I don't care if her father is the deputy mayor, that witch has got serious problems and she should be locked up or seriously medicated or both.

LEEANN: Please. I went through the "I'm as crazy as a French film" years ago. It's so tired.

(Just then, a LOUD SIREN goes off. Everyone looks around. Not alarmed — just annoyed. SQUID, the anti-authority skater punk, jumps out from behind the stacks and runs at the door.)

SQUID: Don't let that door close!

(Squid's too late. Just then, every door, every window, every drawer suddenly LOCKS. We're talking maximum security lockdown here. Silence. Then the intercom kicks on with creepy "soothing music." Everyone stares: this isn't the norm.)

MIA: What the hell was that?!

(The Automated Teacher Unit speaks in pre-recorded fragments, each word at a different pitch.)

AUTOMATED TEACHER UNIT: Mia Safronski, one afternoon detention for unauthorized word.

MIA: But I've got *The Vagina Monologues* audition this afternoon.

AUTOMATED TEACHER UNIT: Mia Safronski, one afternoon detention for inappropriate anatomical reference.

MIA: But it's a play — I truly hate this place.

AUTOMATED TEACHER UNIT: I heard that.

(Mia's about to explode but thinks better of it.)

SQUID: I'll tell you what it was. It's the SS3000 in full lockdown mode. Check the windows and vents. I'll try the doors.

(Squid's the only one in a state of alarm; he checks the perimeter.)

Locked. Locked. Locked.

DARCY: That guy is so—

MORGAN: *(Cutting her off:)* Marlon Brando in *The Wild One?*

(Squid tests the windows.)

SQUID: Locked.

JEREMY: What's going on? My computer's dead.

ROSIE: *(To Jeremy:)* Hey. How long is this going to take? I need a paper on chinchilla mating habits by seventh period.

JEREMY: Don't get your panties in a bunch, ma chère.

ROSIE: What'd you say to me?

JEREMY: *(Frightened:)* We're just having some technical difficulties. We'll be right with you. *(To Vince:)* You're supposed to guard my body, not stand there like a sideshow geek. Now go see if anyone else is having power problems. This thing won't reboot.

(Jeremy goes from computer to computer, trying to get a connection. Squid checks the vents – they're locked too.)

SQUID: They've got the vents too. Hello? Is everyone on Prozac or what?

(Vince tries the library door; it's locked.)

VINCE: Hey, the door's locked.

(Vince runs to another door; it's locked too.)

MIA: What's going on?

VINCE: I don't know. It's like everything's locked up.

SQUID: No wonder people go live in log cabins in the woods.

(Vince and Mia run frantically through the library checking all the same things Squid has already checked. Meanwhile, Leeann files her nails.)

LEEANN: *(To Rosie:)* I love your shoes. Where'd you get those?

ROSIE: In Brooklyn.

LEEANN: Where's that?

ROSIE: In Brooklyn.

LEEANN: Oh, like actual Brooklyn. That's so cool. I've never been to New York. My boyfriend says I've got to go. Though he says I've got more of an LA look so this is where I'll probably work out of. But so many people are bi-coastal these days...   *That?*

(No response.)

So what class is your paper for?

ROSIE: It's for a stupid class taught by a psychotic man with prison tattoos all up and down his arms who has us all researching mating habits of various rodents for reasons entirely unknown to me as we're studying Western Religions.

LEEANN: Oh, Mr. Motor. He's pretty harmless, for the most part. Just don't agree to any extra credit.

ROSIE: I hate this place.

LEEANN: Just 72 more days to go.

ROSIE: Not even. As soon as my boyfriend gets his Camaro running, he's going to drive out here and save me from this nauseating happy-go-lucky mini-skirts-and-jamba-juice-minimall land known as Southern California. All this sunshine makes me want to puke.

LEEANN: *(Not sure how to respond:)* I like Jamba Juice.

(Jeremy can't find a working machine.)

VINCE: Jeremy?

JEREMY: WHAT!

VINCE: Everything's locked. Even the drawers.

MIA: Even the bathroom's locked!

MORGAN: The bathroom's locked?

LEX: The bathroom can't be locked.

(Now everyone is in a tizzy.)

LEEANN: You mean—

VINCE: We're totally locked in here. I mean, like, totally.

LEEANN: I think I'm feeling a nic fit coming on.

(She rummages through her purse.)

Does anyone have a cigarette?

ROSIE: *(To Jeremy:)* Listen, buddy boy, are you still open for business or do I have to go through my other supplier?

JEREMY: Get out of my face, Scary Woman. The internet's down! There's no e-information coming in or going out. Check the phone jacks.

(Vince checks the phones.)

VINCE: The lines are dead.

(Rosie sighs and calls out on her cell phone. No signal.)

ROSIE: Oh great, no signal. This is just what I need. A failing grade from Mr. Motor, the ex-con, rodent-loving, religion teacher. My mother (may she drop dead and rot in hell) is like totally going to cut off my long distance. Does anyone know anything about chinchillas?

ALICE: *(Reciting from memory:)* A squirrel-like rodent (Chinchilla Langier) native to the mountains of South America and widely raised in captivity for its soft, pale gray fur.

PIGEON: Oh, I love chinchillas. *(To the frogs:)* Oh, I love you guys too.

ROSIE: I repeat, I hate this place.

(Jeremy, looking like one of those strung-out stock floor traders, checks all of his phones, pagers, and electronic notebooks.)

JEREMY: I can't even call my broker.

VINCE: Are you OK?

JEREMY: Get off me, you fag.

VINCE: I was just—

JEREMY: Why don't you make yourself useful and tell me what's going on out there.

(Vince shuffles dejectedly to a vent and tries to communicate with the outside world.)

VINCE: Hello... Can anyone hear me? Hello...

(Mia bangs on another vent.)

MIA: Help! We're trapped! Get us out of here!

SQUID: I wouldn't waste your energy.

MIA: And why is that?

SQUID: WAKE UP, EVERYBODY! We're prisoners.

MORGAN: What do you mean prisoners? Like Ingrid Bergman in *Notorious* when the evil German spies started drugging her and Cary Grant didn't even know because they were having this totally ridiculous fight because they didn't realize that they both loved each other and she almost died?

(Mia starts hyperventilating.)

MIA: I just need everyone to know that I'm clinically claustrophobic so if I start banging my head on the wall or writing the same creepy sentence over and over again, just strap me down.

LEX: This isn't an audition, Mia. It's just another computer malfunction.

MIA: Have you ever been trapped in a well-used Port-O-Potty for twelve hours in Tijuana in August?

LEX: Hm...can't say that I have.

MIA: Well, my Aunt Booty was and now she's doing time at the funny farm.

LEX: Calm down. This isn't a Port-O-Potty.

MIA: No. It's bizarro Port-O-Potty. This time the bathroom's locked. What if I have to go? I've got a very small bladder!

(Lex tries to calm a hysterical Mia.)

ROSIE: Oh, brother. Leave it to a bunch of sheltered rich kids in Southern California to freak out about being locked in their fancy school library.

(Distracted by the mania, Simone finally takes off her earphones.)

SIMONE: What's going on?

GARRETT: We're locked in here.

SIMONE: Oh.

(Simone goes back to her music and reading.)

LEX: I'm sure it's just the stupid security system malfunctioning. Like every other brilliant idea the school board has.

MIA: Like when they replaced the nurse with an automated machine and she vaccinated that kid 200 times and he had to go to the hospital?

LEX: OK, that's not a good example. It's more like when they accepted the corporate sponsorship from CliffsNotes and replaced our entire library collection with these noxious ~~yellow~~ brain-drainers.

GARRETT: My favorite was when they banned all sharp objects and we had to write with crayons for a week. Ooh — check out Miss December.

(Garrett shows the magazine. The girls scoff.)

What? She looks like a very interesting woman.

LEX: Someone will get this hunk of junk back on-line and we'll all be fine.

SQUID: This isn't our same-old same-old sucky security system at work here.

LEX: Another conspiracy theory to share with the group, Squid?

SQUID: If anyone bothered to read the School Board minutes, maybe you'd know that they just installed the SS3000. AKA, a little institutional security brought to you by our friends at Northrop. Hello? Does anyone read *anything?* The same people who brought us such useful items as...the Stealth

Bomber? Our tax dollars hard at work to make our children prisoners of our own paranoia.

DARCY: Well, do you know how many tax dollars we spend on graffiti vandals?

SQUID: And do you know how much we pay out in civil liberties when we walk into our school?

(Squid grabs Morgan. She's both repulsed and intrigued: who is this mysterious man?)

Look up there, what do you see?

MORGAN: I think it's that Baywatch dude but I'll have to consult with someone who lived through the early 80s.

SQUID: Look into his eyes.

MORGAN: Oh! Is that—

SQUID: A camera monitor. And look at the 3-D picture of the Big Mac. What's in the center?

MORGAN: Special sauce, lettuce, cheese?

SQUID: Look again. Smile. You're on Invading Our Civil Liberties Camera.

MORGAN: You're crazy. Like James Dean in *Rebel Without A Cause* who was so tortured because he felt different inside and he thought Natalie Wood felt different too and maybe she did but it was too late to save him because he was on a collision course with danger.

SQUID: Maybe I am crazy. Or maybe we're all just one big experiment. Did you know that one of the school's major contributors is a medical research laboratory? Maybe in exchange for our "education," we're giving ourselves up as guinea pigs.

DARCY: Tell it to your parole officer.

SQUID: Just because I'm a delinquent doesn't mean I'm not telling the truth.

MORGAN: Yeah, what kind of name is Squid, anyway?

SQUID: *(Flirting:)* Let's go out some time. I'll show you.

DARCY: ~~Ew! You~~ Keep away from her, ~~you~~ animal!

MORGAN: Yeah!

SQUID: We're all animals, baby. Some of us just pretend we're not.

(Lily suddenly jumps up and sings The Sex Pistols' Anarchy song.)

LILY: *I AM AN ANTI-CHRIST!*
DON'T KNOW WHAT I WANT
BUT I KNOW HOW TO GET IT
CAUSE I...WANNA BE...
ANARCHY!

(Pigeon stares, mouth agape.)

LILY: *(To Pigeon:)* Don't make me eat one of your frogs.

PIGEON: *(To her frogs:)* Shh... It's OK, little guys. She didn't mean it.

LILY: You know, if I had to spend another second in here with you pathetic drones, I think I'd kill myself with a rusty fork.

LEEANN: No one's stopping you.

LILY: Kiss, kiss to you too, Leeann. *(To Garrett:)* What are you looking at, surfer boy?

GARRETT: Why don't you go sacrifice some goats, Freaky Satan Chick?

(Lily stands unsteadily for a moment, then composes herself.)

LILY: That's not bad idea.

(Lily heads for the door and tries to open it. It's locked. She tries again and again.)

The door's locked.

JEREMY: I feel like I'm in a bad *Star Trek* episode.

VINCE: Yeah, maybe there's something out of alignment with the space-time continuum.

JEREMY: You're such a stooge.

VINCE: I'm not a stooge.

JEREMY: Stooge.

LILY: What's going on?

MIA: We're prisoners of war. We can't get into the bathroom. But hey, it's more material for my method acting class so what do I care? As long as my bladder holds out and I don't explode all over the library walls.

LEX: Breathe, Mia. Breathe.

(Mia practices her breathing.)

LILY: You mean I'm stuck in here with you parasitic zombies?

(Lily stands unsteadily for a moment, looks around, then pounces on Simone's CD player.)

SIMONE: What the —

(Lily plugs herself in and starts rocking to the music.)

Hey. That's mine. Give it back.

(Simone tries to take the CD player back. Lily lashes out and growls menacingly. Simone gets out of the way — fast.)

Did you see that? She tried to bite me. I swear to God, that girl tried to bite me.

LEEANN: Great! We're locked in the library with government-issued security, Crazy Lily went rabid, and I only have half a piece of Nicorette.

(A STRANGE, MUFFLED NOISE from the vent.)

DARCY: Did you hear that?

MORGAN: I think it's coming from the vent.

JEREMY: Vince. Check it out.

MORGAN: This is so *The Haunting.* (The original, that is, not the cheesy re-make.)

MIA: This is so freaking me out.

SIMONE: This is so Jean-Paul Sartre it isn't even funny.

(Vince scrambles up to the vent to listen again. The MUFFLED NOISE.)

MIA: What the hell —

LEEANN: Shhh!

(Vince stands paralyzed. On his face, a look of fear and confusion. Silence.)

JEREMY: Well? What was it?

VINCE: I think...

JEREMY: What!

VINCE: I think...

(He tries to hold back tears.)

JEREMY: Come on, you fag, spit it out.

VINCE: You know...I REALLY DON'T LIKE IT WHEN YOU CALL ME THAT.

ALICE: It was the kind of normal you don't recognize as normal until things aren't normal anymore...if that makes any sense.

JEREMY: Who told Dictionary Girl to talk?

ALICE: It was just a day. I guess you'd call it average. Like one of those days when you're complaining about how unfair the geometry final was and what a pain in the ass that kid Lance is and when you go home and your parents ask how school was, you just shrug your shoulders and turn on the television to watch some stupid rendition of teen life written by some burned out forty-something guy from LA. It was just...normal. And then you hear this noise. I would say gunfire but that's not what it sounds like because it's not like it sounds in the movies. And normal is turned inside out like one of those frogs in biology class. You don't know what's happening but you do know it's bad and you do know right then and there that it's going to take years to recover from this. You're like: this is traumatic. I'm experiencing trauma. And it races through your body like this terrible disease. Your heart is in your throat and you think you're going to choke to death if it beats again. And then you get this rush of adrenaline. Like those animals on National Geographic who suddenly realize that they're surrounded. Your legs start moving. You're running faster than you've ever run before. You don't even know where. You're doing this thing called saving your life and your brain is completely off-line. And all of a sudden there are these people there holding you and telling you it's over. They're shoving pamphlets in your hands about Why Bad Things Happen to Good People. And Where Was God? Your teachers and your parents and all the politicians are saying that you need to talk about this. And the only thing you want to do is watch that teen show written by the burned out LA guy and laugh at those evil cheerleader witches. But even he's sobered up and he's writing about trauma and violence and how to process pain. There's nowhere to go to escape it. Except in your head. So you decide to pass the time reading the dictionary and hope to hell that you'll feel better about life before you hit zýzzyra, but you always keep your running shoes handy just in case you hear the noise again. Just in case you have to run for your life.

GARRETT: Well, that really clears things up.

LEX: Shut up, Garrett.

GARRETT: What?

JEREMY: Can someone please translate for me?

MORGAN: I think she's talking about the shooting at that school last year.

JEREMY: OK, my next question would be: why?

GARRETT: Or perhaps the question is: why not?

MIA: What's going on? Why are we talking about this?

VINCE: I think...someone's been shot.

(No one knows what to do or say. Blackout.)

SCENE 2

(Lights up. Later. The clock reads 3:40 PM. Everyone's numb and on edge. Alice comes to. Lex tends to her.)

ALICE: Where am I?

LEX: We're still at school.

ALICE: Where's my dictionary?

(Pigeon fetches the dictionary.)

PIGEON: Here you go.

(Alice clutches the dictionary like it's a stuffed animal.)

Is she...going to be OK?

MIA: Yeah. If you think little padded rooms in institutions where you can't wear shoe laces is OK.

LEX: She'll be fine. It's just her body's way of dealing with stress.

(Darcy and Morgan are back on poster detail.)

DARCY: Come on, Pigeon.   Posters don't just hang themselves.

PIGEON: Oh. OK. I've got to—

LEX: Maybe she doesn't want to help perpetuate an institution that gives horny vodka-guzzling baboons the right to grope, puke on, and generally manhandle cookie-cut-out Barbie wannabes in tight taffeta dresses.

MORGAN: What's wrong, Lex? Going stag?

DARCY: It's called a prom, for your information, and 99.9% of people have this thing called "fun." You should try it.

LEX: Isn't that the same delusional percentage who think that high school represents the best times of their life?

PIGEON: Uh... It's OK. I like to help.

(Pigeon goes to work on the posters. Leeann paints her toenails.)

LEEANN: I can't believe this is happening here. I mean, this is the kind of thing you watch on TV. And you're like: those poor people.

VINCE: I wonder if our parents are watching this on TV right now.

LEEANN: I wonder if they're going to try to interview us and everything.

MIA: Yeah, Leeann, maybe it's your big break.

LEEANN: I've already got an agent. How about you?

(Jeremy looks out the window.)

JEREMY: No, look. It's a total ghost town out there. No way someone's been shot. This place would be swarming with cops and reporters.

MIA: I wish someone would make an announcement or something.

(Mia bangs on the vent.)

We're in here! Get us out of here!

VINCE: What are you doing? What if he's still out there? What if everyone is dead and he's going from room to room looking for more innocent people to kill? Did you think about that? Maybe we're just better off being quiet.

MIA: And what if there's no one out there and you just heard it wrong?

JEREMY: Maybe it's too much Mortal Kombat messing with your brain.

LEEANN: Yeah. What do you mean you *think* someone was shot? There's not a lot of gray area there. I mean, what exactly did you hear?

VINCE: There was this...strange noise...and then —

JEREMY: What kind of strange noise?

VINCE: It was...really...loud and...sudden.

LEEANN: Was it like a car backfiring?

MIA: Yeah. Maybe it was a car backfiring.

VINCE: No, it was different. It was —

JEREMY: You're not giving us a lot to go on.

VINCE: I heard someone scream.

MORGAN: Was it a man or a woman?

VINCE: I'm not sure.

JEREMY: Come on, was it high or low?

VINCE: I can't remember. It happened so fast.

GARRETT: Was it —

(He screams.)

LEEANN: Or —

(She screams.)

JEREMY: Or maybe it was —

(He screams.)

MIA: Or —

(She screams.)

VINCE: I KNOW WHAT I HEARD.

GARRETT: OK...I'm glad we got that settled.

(Rosie tries the bathroom door again.)

ROSIE: Does anyone have the key for this thing? Hey. What are we supposed to do if we have to go? Hello?

(Squid holds out a can of Coke.)

SQUID: You can borrow this.

ROSIE: I knew I shouldn't have come in the stupid library. Open up!

(Garrett spritzes his mouth with breath freshener and approaches Rosie.)

GARRETT: Step aside, damsel in distress. *(Trying the door:)* Hm. This is locked.

ROSIE: Thanks for the Obvious Report.

GARRETT: Hey, uh, maybe after we get out of here we could —

ROSIE: My boyfriend can bench press 225 pounds.

GARRETT: OK...I'll see ya around.

(Simone's still reading. Mia approaches.)

MIA: How can you just sit there and read?

SIMONE: What should I do?

MIA: I don't know. Have a reaction?

SIMONE: Should I hug you and cry and pretend that we actually like each other?

MIA: You know what's wrong with this world?

SIMONE: People like you think you know what's wrong with this world?

MIA: What is your problem?

SIMONE: I don't have one. Life sucks and then you die. So this moment is no better or worse than the next moment.

MIA: And I suppose if someone ran in here with a gun, you'd just sit there and read your stupid book.

SIMONE: It's Jean Paul Sartre's *No Exit.*

MIA: *(Imitates the French, badly:)* Whatever that is.

SIMONE: Read much? It's about three people who don't know each other and don't like each other and they're locked in this room together. Only it's not an ordinary room. It's hell. And they're never going to get out. Ironic, huh?

MIA: I just think it's really sad how much you hate yourself.

SIMONE: I don't hate myself. I'm just not hung up on death. That's the problem with the world. Everyone is so afraid of death, life becomes a living hell. Why do you think people buy guns and shoot each other?

MIA: And I guess you think it's OK just to run around killing people?!

SIMONE: No, I'm just saying I understand the urge!

GARRETT: Girls, GIRLS! Let's put our claws away. No cat fights allowed in the library. Wait a minute, everyone. Genius has struck. If only we had a giant pit of Jello we could have girl-on-girl wrestling.

(The intercom kicks on.)

PRINCIPAL'S VOICE: Everything is fine. I repeat, everything is fine.

LEX: See?

(Then, a song from The Sound of Music plays over the intercom.)

SQUID: And the hills are alive with the sound of music.

DARCY: Was that Principal Walters?

MORGAN: It didn't sound like Principal Walters.

LEEANN: Maybe he's being held hostage.

MIA: Maybe he's been killed.

SQUID: We can always hope.

(Pause while people take this in.)

DARCY: You better take that back.

SQUID: What.

DARCY: That's an incredibly inappropriate, insensitive, and, and, and unpatriotic thing to say.

SQUID: *(With Hitler salute:)* Yes, mon Fürer!

DARCY: *(Aghast:)* The last thing we need at a time like this is sarcasm.

SIMONE: Yeah, and while we're at it, let's get rid of the poets, philosophers, and those pesky Jews.

DARCY: *(More aghast-ness:)* I am trying to give us direction and purpose to guide us through this difficult time. It is imperative that we stand unified against evil-doers and remember who we are and what we're made of.

SQUID: And who put you in charge?

DARCY: The student body did, mister.

SQUID: We're not falling for that old line anymore. We all know the real question is: who won the popular vote?

GARRETT: I call for a new vote!

LEX: Yeah. Just because you're president out there, doesn't mean you should be president in here.

DARCY: What are you talking about?   I won!   I'm the president!

SIMONE: You do know you're not a real President, right?

GARRETT: New vote! New vote! New vote!
(People chant along.) LEX, MIA, SQUID, MORGAN

DARCY: Fine!   You want one of these losers to be your president, be my guest.   Let's see...should it be the Satan worshiper or the juvenile delinquent?   Hmm...

MORGAN: Oo! I'll run.

DARCY: Perfect!   Let's have Morgan in charge and if something really terrible happens, she can tell us which Hello Kitty accessories to wear.   She won't know thing number one about the code book or about evacuation procedure, but she will be able to reference stupid old movies that no one in this generation has heard of until we all go clinically insane!

SQUID: (Sneezes to cover:) ~~Bitch.~~ JERK.

GARRETT: OK. My money's on Darcy in the Jello pit.

(Morgan tries hard not to cry.)

MORGAN: You're ∧GARRETT just like that evil woman in *All About Eve* who acts like she's everybody's best friend and all the time, she's really sabotaging everyone and in the end she becomes this famous star but she's all alone and everyone hates her because she'll do anything to claw her way to the top.

SQUID: I saw that.

MORGAN: Yeah, Bette Davis kicked ass, didn't she?

LEEANN: I think Darcy's right. ~~Not about being a bitch, but~~ we need someone in charge figuring out how to get out of here. No offense to you all, but I've got a screening to get to.

ROSIE: *(To Squid:)* What about you?

SQUID: Who...me?

ROSIE: You're all acting like you know what's going on.

SQUID: Nothing we can do but wait. It's all a part of...The Experiment.

ROSIE: What are you, the eccentric cry-for-help cousin from Disney Teen Crap TV or something?

SQUID: What? We're locked in by the Department of Defense. You can't just trip the locks.

JEREMY: Yes, you can.

(Everyone looks at Jeremy.)

Code is man-made and what is man-made is made to be broken.

ROSIE: Well, get to it, computer geek.

JEREMY: Hacker. I'm a hacker, thank you very much.

ROSIE: Open the door and I'll call you the Dali Lama.

SQUID: That's funny. I thought people who programmed the intercom system to burp the Star Spangled Banner were called *crackers*, not hackers.

GARRETT: You did that? That was a good one. I really appreciated the humor in that.

JEREMY: Oh yeah? You show me a cracker who can set up and run a modified UNIX system without any help. It's the hackers of this world who built the internet. It's the hackers who make the global economy spin. It's like one gigantic spider web out there and it's the hackers who are the silk spinners. Without us, the world as we know it would cease to exist.

ROSIE: What are you? Superman's arch villain? We don't need to take over the world, we need to open the friggin' door.

JEREMY: Come on, Vince. Let's crack this walnut.

(Vince doesn't move.)

Yo, earth to Vince. Hey, gay boy. Quit your crying and let's get moving.

LEX: He said don't call him that.

JEREMY: Why don't you shave your armpits and stay out of it.

LEX: Because I can't tolerate little men with little egos taking their little aggressions out on other people because they just don't—how do you say—measure up? And if I have to skip all my classes and fail out of school just so I can follow you around, I'll do it. And the next time I hear one of those little remarks coming out of your little mouth, I'll teach you a lesson the old fashioned way.

LEEANN: You go, girl.

JEREMY: What is it, gay pride day? Whatever. I don't need anyone's help. Never have, never will.

(Jeremy drags out his laptop and starts to tap away. Everyone's quiet except Lily who croons to her music.)

PIGEON: Maybe...someone should...tell her...what's going on...

GARRETT: Count me out.

SIMONE: Get my CD player back while you're at it.

LEEANN: It's not like she's going to care.

LEX: How do you know?

LEEANN: I've known that girl since we were in pre-school and the only thing she cares about is pissing off her parents because she thinks they owe her.

SQUID: For what? Having so much money?

LEEANN: How should I know? But I swear, every year it's a new thing. Last year it was Jesus; this year it's Satan. Totally freaks out her parents.

LEX: I'll tell her.

(Lex approaches, Lily continues to sing, completely oblivious. Lex taps her on the shoulder.)

LILY: What do you want?

LEX: We just thought you should know what's going on.

(No response.)

LEX: Well. We're locked in the library and —

LILY: I know that.

LEX: And...Vince thinks he may have heard a gunshot. We don't know for sure what's happened, but it doesn't look good.

(Lily suddenly pops to her feet.)

LILY: Are you happy about this, Lex?

LEX: What?

LILY: We all know about your *ways*.

LEX: Whatever. Now you know.

(Lex walks away but Lily aggressively pursues her.)

LILY: Sounds to me like God is sick and tired of people like you running around acting any old way you please.

MIA: You don't know anything about God, Lily. So why don't you shut up?

LEEANN: Yeah. The *Children of the Corn* routine is wearing way thin.

LILY: Sounds to me like your little God has given up on all you Pop 40 pukes.

(Lily becomes increasingly belligerent, her speech slurred.)

Think about it. The shootings? The bombings? The germ warfare? This is it. This is the end. And you know what? I'm GLAD. I'm so sick of this place.

(Garrett tries to escort her away.)

GARRETT: OK, back into the drunk tank with you.

(As she continues to rant, Garrett and others begin to boo. Darcy, meanwhile, tries to quiet people down. This is a library after all.)

LILY: Everyone can just blow each other up for all I care. Tell the terrorists we're over here. Tell the off-balance lunatics living in the woods, tell all the serial-killers, and the Neo-Nazi rednecks that their day has come. They. Shall. Inherit. The Earth. Because your God gave up on you so long ago, you can't even remember what He looks like.

(Lily's drowned out.)

LEEANN: I told you.

(Darcy inspects the Automated Teacher Unit.)

DARCY: Oh. My. God. Someone has tampered with the Automated Teacher Unit. I wonder who that was...Squid?

That's a Class One offense, you know. Mandatory suspension.
It's in the student handbook.

*(Darcy knocks the side of the Automated Teacher which revs
back up.)*

AUTOMATED TEACHER UNIT: Mia Safronski, one
afternoon detention... Mia Safronski, one afternoon
detention... *(etc.)*

MIA: Why is that thing always picking on me?

DARCY: If someone doesn't confess to this act of overt
vandalism, I will be forced to take down everyone's name.

GARRETT: Shut that thing up, Darcy.

ROSIE: Yeah. Or I'll do it for you.

DARCY: So be it. Everyone will suffer because of one person's
cowardice.

*(Darcy writes down names. Simone gets up and walks over to
the A.T.)*

Ah, Simone... Do you have something to confess?

SIMONE: Yeah. I confess this noise irritates me.

(Simone wails on the A.T. with a giant SAT prep book.)

DARCY: Hey—you can't do that.

SIMONE: But I can. Look.

(Simone smacks the A.T. again and again.)

DARCY: That is...so...against the rules.

SIMONE: Rules? Whose rules? Their rules? I don't really
care about *their* rules any more. I'm only interested in *my*
rules. And it's against *my* rules to lock us in the library for
hours and hours. And it's against *my* rules to spy on us with

hidden cameras, to search our lockers with police dogs, and to monitor drug use through modern toilet technology.

DARCY: Step away from the A.T. or I will be forced to report your destructive and antisocial behaviors to the school counselor.

SIMONE: Do you know what else is against my rules? Annoying nitpicking rule hounds are against my rules. I'm afraid I have to report anyone who reports anyone because I am morally offended by tow-the-line tattletales.

GARRETT: Whoee! I'll tell you all what, I can't promise that I'll get you guys out of here but once we're out, I'll throw the best party you've ever seen. And you better believe we'll have barely clad ladies in a giant pit of Jello fighting like cats all night long.

LEX: Does every word that comes out of your mouth have to be so sexist?

GARRETT: Oh, yeah. And one lesbian lumberjack for Lex Luther.

(Lex tries to control her anger.)

LEX: You are so painfully ignorant, I almost feel sorry for you.

(It doesn't work. She smacks him. They struggle. Total cacophony.)

PIGEON: Oh. Hey. Come on. Hey. You guys.

GARRETT: You're pretty strong for a girl.

MIA: You get him, Lex.

SQUID: Anarchy!

DARCY: Fisticuffs in the library is a Class Two offense.

MORGAN: Girl power!

VINCE: Would you quit making so much noise. He'll hear us.

PIGEON: WHY DOESN'T EVERYONE JUST SHUT UP?

(Lex and Garrett stop fighting. Everyone looks, stunned, at Pigeon.)

GARRETT: The Pigeon has spoken.

PIGEON: I'm sorry. I don't...usually...yell.

GARRETT: I hereby nominate The Pigeon to be our interim president.

LEEANN: Damn, I second the nomination.

GARRETT: Speech. Speech!

(Everyone looks at Pigeon who is so shy she looks like she's in physical pain.)

PIGEON: We've got to stop...being so mean...to each other.

(Pause. Is that it?)

GARRETT: Yeah! Sing it, sister!

(Garrett cheers, gets the crowd going.)

Go on, Pigeon. Impress us with your knowledge of the animal kingdom.

PIGEON: Um...I think that, you know, ants. They work together to protect their colony. And the bees? Same thing. They are very socialist in a way. Not that I'm saying we should be socialists or communists. Well, I'm not crazy about capitalism. But these models...learn from them...we can.

GARRETT: Yoda has spoken! Yoda! Yoda!

(Some cheers, some laughs. Pigeon realizes she's the butt of the joke.)

PIGEON: *(To her frogs:)* Oh, hello Bert. You want an olive, boy? Yeah. That's good.

ALICE: For your information, her name is Sophie.

VINCE: And just because someone's quiet or, you know, a dork, doesn't mean we don't have feelings too. I mean, they.

GARRETT: What is this, an after school special? I was just trying to lighten the mood. It's our duty during this trying time to crack jokes. Right, President Pigeon?

PIGEON: Sam? Are you OK? Does anyone have any water? I think there's something wrong with Sam. Just hold on a little longer, little buddy.

GARRETT: That was "yes" in Pigeon.

DARCY: Stop it, Garrett.

GARRETT: Or what? Are you *so* going to report me?

DARCY: You know, Pigeon—I mean, Sophie—may not be the best public speaker and she may have frogs in all her pockets and she may be so quiet it's kinda creepy, but some day we're going to be reading about that nature freak hugging an endangered tree or saving a baby seal.

MORGAN: Yeah, she's going to make a difference out there.

DARCY: And that's a lot more than we can say for you.

GARRETT: Jeez. Is like every girl in this library on the rag, or what?

(Now Rosie is playing tug of war with the bathroom door and barely able to keep from crying.)

ROSIE: Open up, damn it. Open up this damned door.

(Something smacks against the other side of the door.)

KATARINA: *(From bathroom:)* Leave me alone!

ROSIE: Oh my God.   I think there's someone locked in the bathroom.

MIA: It *is* the Port-O-Potty.   Don't worry, we'll get you out.

ROSIE: This is weird.   It feels like someone's holding it shut. Come on, help me pull it.

(Mia helps pull the door.)

MIA: Yeah, it's not locked. She's holding it shut. Come on, we need one more person.

(Morgan gets in there to help.)

ROSIE: OK, on three.

MIA: One, two, THREE.

(They all pull hard on the door. Out flies Katrina, the substitute teacher who's had a hell of a day.)

ROSIE: *(Running into bathroom:)* Thank you, God.

KATARINA: Keep away from me! You're all animals!

(Blackout.)

SCENE 3

(The clock reads 5:10 PM. Everyone now sits in rows of seats — very organized. Each person has a paper taped to their shirt with his/her proper name written on it. Katarina, still shaking and upset, sits at the front of the room. Leeann coughs — a smoker's cough. Katarina stares at her.)

LEEANN: Sorry.

(Everyone waits. The intercom comes on with The Principal's voice — which is becoming more degraded each time we hear it. Katarina jumps.)

PRINCIPAL'S VOICE: Everything is fine. I repeat, everything is fine.

(The MUSIC kicks on again. Katarina goes over and tries the door again. It's still locked.)

KATARINA: *(Mumbling under her breath:)* Yeah, right. Everything's fine. Except I'm still locked in here with these animals. I better be getting overtime for this.

(As she passes Garrett, he looks at her.)

What are you looking at?

GARRETT: I was just — Nothing.

(Garrett looks ahead. The intercom clicks on again.)

PRINCIPAL'S VOICE: Everything is fine. I repeat, everything is fine.

(The MUSIC. Katarina's had it. She slides the desk over to the intercom, gets up, and smacks it to death with her shoe. The music gurgles to a stop.)

VINCE: But what if —

(Katarina whips around and looks at Vince sternly.)

Nothing.

(Blackout.)

SCENE 4

(The clock now reads 9:30 PM. Everyone sits in the same position – looking more haggard, tired, and cramped. People exchange looks but are helpless to do anything as Katarina keeps an eagle eye watch. Squid raises his hand. He's got it raised for quite some time before Katarina acknowledges him.)

KATARINA: Roger.

SQUID: Actually, I go by –

KATARINA: Roger.

SQUID: OK...I've got this cramp in my leg and it's hurting real bad due to this skating injury I got when I popped an ollie and the board didn't and I dislocated my kneecap. You should have seen the X-Ray, the doctor was like –

KATARINA: Get to the point.

SQUID: I was wondering if I could stand up to stretch said leg due to said injury to...said...leg...please.

(Morgan laughs, Katarina whirls around.)

KATARINA: Was your hand raised?

MORGAN: No.

KATARINA: Did I call on you?

MORGAN: No.

KATARINA: Then why is noise coming out of your mouth?

MORGAN: Because I'm like the against-the-system trouble-making delinquents in *Blackboard Jungle*?

KATARINA: You think you're so funny?

MORGAN: Uh...

KATARINA: You're going to get eaten alive out there.

All of you.
You think you're on top of the world here. You think you can be so sarcastic and get all up in people's faces. Out there? You're nothing. Out there?
You are going to cry like babies.
When you can't make your rent.
When your utilities are overdue.
When you don't have health insurance and you get this terrible infection and you have to go to the free clinic and you have to wait for three hours with all the winos, runaways, and drug addicts to get some really terrible medical care and free antibiotics.
Then you're going to call Mom and Dad in tears. And you know what they're going to do?
They're going to Cut You Off. They're going to decide that you're old enough to support yourself. They're going to sell the house you grew up in, they're going to sell all of your childhood belongings, and then they're going to go on a world cruise. And you know what? You're not going to have the energy to make all your bratty remarks because you're going to be too busy thinking about how you're going to feed yourself on three dollars a day.

(A NOISE.)

Who was that?

(Silence.)

Who. Was. That?

(Pigeon raises her hand.)

PIGEON: I'm sorry...I usually...I don't...but sometimes...and then...well...OK.

KATARINA: What?

PIGEON: My stomach growled.

KATARINA: Oh.

PIGEON: I'm sorry.

KATARINA: Right. Right.

(Katarina seems to come to — as if waking from the nightmare of her day.)

What time is it?

DARCY: 9:30 PM.

KATARINA: Guess it's way past dinner time. Anyone hungry?

(Everyone's hand goes up.)

Here's what we're going to do. Let's pool our resources — I'm talking anything remotely resembling food — and divide it up evenly among the group. Who knows when these morons are going to find us? If they ever do. I mean, these people in charge of educating you? Simple-minded bureaucratic ghouls. They probably need to fill out some form in triplicate before they can unlock the door. But they don't even have the right form so they'll need to requisition one from the district office. And it will take some disgruntled office worker two to fifty-two weeks to process the request. And if they have the right form in stock then they'll tape it on to the back of an extremely stupid turtle and send it to you right away. At this point, of course, we'll all be dead so it doesn't really matter. But I digress. What were we talking about?

(Alice raises her hand.)

Yeah.

ALICE: I've got some apple slices.

KATARINA: Great. Bring everything up here and anyone who hoards gets hit fifty times with an SAT prep book.

(Silence – mortified looks.)

That was a joke.

(Phew. Everyone [except Lily] searches their pockets and backpacks for anything resembling food. Lily sits still, staring glassy-eyed ahead.)

SQUID: I'd like to present the Slim Jim variety pack: Teriyaki, Spicy Beef, and half a BBQ Chicken. I highly recommend the chicken. It's got the tang, with no chemical aftertaste.

VINCE: Meatball Stroganoff.

MORGAN: I've got these really cool Japanese chewy candies in shrimp, sake, or seaweed flavors.

SIMONE: Twinkie.

MIA: Bubble Burger.

ROSIE: Doritoes.

DARCY: Toblerone.

JEREMY: I've got— Oh, forget it. I think this is part of my TV.

GARRETT: Altoids, Certs, and Binaca.

KATARINA: Subtle.

GARRETT: As the Boy Scouts always say...

LEEANN: I've got half a piece of Nicorette. I was saving it for a real emergency. But...well, it's my contribution.

LEX: I've got half a wheat-free sugar-free all-organic apple bar.

GARRETT: Yum.

PIGEON: I've got an olive. Oop. Sam, give that back. Sam... I'm sorry. Here, let me clean that. He's had a difficult day. He's usually much better behaved. Shh.

KATARINA: Why don't you keep that? Sam has to eat too. And I've got...a head of lettuce. Don't ask.

MIA: Don't you have anything to put in the pot, Lily?

MORGAN: Yeah. Quit being so *Sierra Madre* and give us your food. What's that?

(Morgan grabs a silver wrapper from her – trying to avoid being bitten.)

Score. Cinnamon Poptart.

(Katarina and others divvy up the food.)

Man, that girl is so *The Three Faces of Eve.*

SQUID: *(Trying to be casual:)* Hey, uh, you ever seen this movie called *Eraserhead*?

MORGAN: I don't think so.

SQUID: You haven't seen *Eraserhead*?! David Lynch's first movie? Oh my God. Check it out. There's this amazing scene with this lady tap-dancing, OK? *Inside* a radiator. She's singing this weird song and all of a sudden these things that look like giant sperm start falling from the ceiling.

MORGAN: Definitely haven't seen that.

SQUID: Yeah, well, you know, that may be your thing or it may not be your thing. I know you're into the movie thing but I don't know if it's just a classic thing or –

MORGAN: Shut up, Squid.

SQUID: OK.

MORGAN: Maybe we could do a double-feature some time.

SQUID: I can dig it.

KATARINA: Dinner time! Come and get it!

(Everyone [except Lily] retrieves their dinner goodies. They stare in disbelief, then their hunger takes over and they snarf it down. For the first moment in a while, everyone seems relaxed.)

GARRETT: Who knew Beef Jerky and Bubble Burger went so well together?

LEEANN: I think the gum really brings out the barbecue flavor.

JEREMY: I'd like to see what the Iron Chef could do with these ingredients. *(To Vince:)* You remember the Wonder Bread episode?

VINCE: Yeah.

JEREMY: You OK?

VINCE: Yeah.

JEREMY: You sure?

VINCE: Yeah. Couldn't be better. Thanks for the concern.

(Vince gets up and walks away.)

DARCY: I wonder who got voted off Survivor tonight.

LEEANN: I hope it was that slut, Tammy.

GARRETT: Hey, don't talk bad about my girl Tammy. She's got the nicest pair of...uh, sunglasses. Did you see those...sunglasses?

SQUID: Yeah...those were some perky...sunglasses.

MORGAN: I like Drake. He kind of reminds me of Robert Mitchum.

MIA: No way, he's so full of himself and ugh! That chest hair is always flapping all around.

SQUID: Annette is clearly going to be the winner. I mean, you guys know these things are rigged, right?

PIGEON: Oh, Annette is so knowledgeable about the local habitat.

ROSIE: Na-uh-uh. It's gonna be that chick Vanessa because if you can survive high school in Fort Greene, you can survive a bunch of horny dorks on network television.

LEX: I can't believe you guys watch that stuff. It's so demeaning.

SIMONE: You have to admit, it's a perfect testimonial to how little we've learned.

LEX: True.

SIMONE: Besides, Tammy is a slut.

(Alice sits with Katarina.)

ALICE: Are you OK?

KATARINA: Yeah. I mean, it's been years, literally years, since I've eaten a Twinkie. Or, one fifteenth of a Twinkie. It's for the best, really. Any more and I would just bloat right up.

ALICE: I was in the sewing class.

KATARINA: Oh.

ALICE: I'm sorry about what they did — about what *we* did.

KATARINA: Call it one of the challenges of substitute teaching.

ALICE: And I'm sorry I didn't do anything.

KATARINA: What could you have done?

ALICE: I could have told them to stop.

KATARINA: They might have tied you up too.

ALICE: That's what I always tell myself. Someone else will do it. I've got my own problems. But it's just a cop-out because I'm afraid. Not of being tied up. But of people looking at me. But next time, I'm going to say something. And I don't care what they think of me.

KATARINA: There's no next time for me. I'm going to grad school. This "living life" thing is for the birds.

GARRETT: Hey. There's an extra helping. Who didn't get theirs?

VINCE: Lily's not eating hers.

MIA: Oh brother. Here we go again.

GARRETT: Hey. Crazy Lily. Your dinner's ready.

(No response. Lily just stares forward.)

LEEANN: Just leave it. She'll get it when she's ready.

KATARINA: What's her deal?

ALICE: Same as all of us. Except she's a personal friend of Satan's.

(Garrett shakes Lily.)

GARRETT: Lily? The Prince of Darkness is going to eat your dinner...

(Lily flops over.)

OH MY GOD. OH MY GOD. OH MY GOD.

LEEANN: She's just being dramatic. Eat your stupid food, Lily.

GARRETT: No. I think there's something SERIOUSLY wrong with her.

MIA: Oh my God.

(Katarina runs over.)

KATARINA: The fun never stops today.

GARRETT: Is this a whatchamacallit. A seizure?

KATARINA: I don't know. Has anyone seen a seizure before?

PIGEON: I gave a squirrel CPR once.

KATARINA: OK, OK, OK.   Let's...lie   her   down and...and...and...

(They try to lie Lily down, her body's rigid.)

GARRETT: She's fighting us.

KATARINA: Lily? Lily? Can you hear us?

GARRETT: Oh man, this is so messed up.

(Katarina listens to her breathing, feels her pulse.)

KATARINA: I don't even know what I'm doing. Uh...uh...uh... Medical dictionary. Someone find a medical dictionary.

LEX: In the CliffsNotes Library? You've got to be kidding me.

ALICE: I've got one. Hey, you never know.

(Alice gets her medical dictionary.)

KATARINA: What about the computers? Can we get on-line yet?

JEREMY: I got as far as the mainframe, but I'm going to need Vince's help to tap into an outside line.

KATARINA: Vince?

(No response.)

JEREMY: Come on, I need your help.

VINCE: You're the hacker.

JEREMY: What are you talking about? What's the big deal—you know I didn't mean that stuff. OK. You know my UNIX system would be nothing without you. There. I said it.

VINCE: Damn right.

JEREMY: Now are you going to help me or not?

VINCE: Let's do it.

(Vince and Jeremy are on it.)

KATARINA: Does anyone know anything about her?

LEEANN: I've known her since forever.

KATARINA: Does she have any medical conditions?

LEEANN: Not that I know of. But—I guess we're not all that close. Is she going to be OK?

GARRETT: Oh my God.

MIA: We're locked in the library and she's going to die.

GARRETT: And then she's going to be dead.

MIA: And then we're all going to be messed up in the head.

GARRETT: Hey—that rhymed.

KATARINA: Someone shut them up.

(Lex and Leeann take care of Mia and Garrett.)

LEX: Don't make us lock you in the bathroom.

LEEANN: I think this is a job for Nicorette.

ROSIE: I feel like an idiot just standing here.

PIGEON: Is there anything we can do?

KATARINA: Check the cell phones again.

(Rosie checks hers. No signal, still.)

ROSIE: Nothing.

KATARINA: Come on, Lily. Wake up. This is going to look very bad on my record.

ROSIE: *(Crossing herself:)* Oh my God.

MORGAN: This is so...

SQUID: Yeah.

(Morgan and Squid hold hands.)

SIMONE: Diabetes.

KATARINA: What?

SIMONE: An insulin attack. It's got to be.

KATARINA: How do you know?

SIMONE: My brother has it. See if she's got a Medic Alert bracelet.

KATARINA: Yeah. Diabetes.

ALICE: *(Reading her medical dictionary:)* OK, I've got something under diabetes. Um... hypoglycemia... low level of glucose...Um... Treatment. "If you are prone to hypoglycemia attacks, you should carry glucose tablets, sugar lumps, or candy. At the first sign of an attack, eat some until you feel normal again, which should be in a few minutes."

MORGAN: I'm the one who stole her poptart.

KATARINA: Someone get the Twinkie, stat.

(Pigeon runs for the Twinkie and hands it to Katarina.)

ALICE: "However..."

KATARINA: What "however"? "However" what?

ALICE: "They should never try to feed you if you become totally unconscious because this could choke you."

KATARINA: Bad Twinkie. No Twinkie. OK. Wait. I know this. Diabetes...

SQUID: The islets of Langerhans —

MORGAN: *(Wiggling her fingers:)* The little finger-like things in the pancreas.

DARCY: Right. They produce insulin. In someone who's diabetic...

LEX: The body doesn't produce it so you have to do injections.

KATARINA: Well, you're actually learning something here. That's a relief. So she needs an injection. Where's her backpack? She must have uh...injectables with her.

(Everyone runs around looking.) —(Leann picks up Lily's backpack)
LEEANN: Does this belong to anyone?

(No response.)

KATARINA: Look inside. Anything...medical looking?

(Leeann looks in the backpack.)

LEEANN: It's like a pharmacy in here.

VINCE: We've got an outside line.

JEREMY: I'm typing in the website. Searching...

LEEANN: Here's something. It looks like a schedule.

LEX: Yeah, look. She had an insulin injection scheduled for 3PM.

KATARINA: So...we give her a shot of insulin?

SIMONE: I think if her blood sugar is this low she needs glucose.

KATARINA: Are you sure?

SIMONE: I think so.

SQUID: That makes sense. Insulin is the hormone that tells the body to produce glucose.

PIGEON: If she's this low, maybe the hormone takes too long.

ROSIE: Yeah, maybe she needs the sugar right in her blood stream.

KATARINA: Um...what does Google say?

JEREMY: Still connecting.

VINCE: There's bad traffic out there.

KATARINA: I hate the internet.

ALICE: I've got it. Under Professional Help it says: "the physician will give you a shot of glucose in a vein in your arm. This works so quickly that you may regain consciousness while the injection is still in progress."

KATARINA: I like the sound of that. Which one's the glucose?

SIMONE: It's...this one.

KATARINA: The syringe?

SIMONE: Yeah.

KATARINA: So I just poke her with this thing?

SIMONE: Yeah.

KATARINA: Are you sure?

SIMONE: You already asked that.

KATARINA: It's just I just have this thing about needles in that...uh...they make me vomit and faint and sometimes I break out in hives and did I mention the vomit?

SIMONE: I'll do it.

(Simone sets up the syringe.)

KATARINA: Anything, boys?

JEREMY: Still connecting.

KATARINA: Great.

SIMONE: Ready.

KATARINA: Are you sure?

SIMONE: Yes.

(Simone gives Lily the shot. Everyone waits silently to see what happens.)

MIA: What if we killed her?

GARRETT: We totally killed her.

LEEANN: Shut up.

LEX: She's going to be fine.

LEEANN: She has to be.

ROSIE: Please, God, let her be OK.

(Lily stirs. She's very groggy.)

LILY: What are you all looking at?

(Everyone cheers.)

JEREMY: We're in.

VINCE: Nope. Connection failed.

KATARINA: Forget it, boys. The internet failed us once again.

LEEANN: Should we give her some food?

SIMONE: No sugar though. She needs protein.

LEEANN: Does a Slim Jim count?

SIMONE: I guess.

(Leeann brings the food to Lily.)

LEEANN: We saved some processed meat product for you.

LILY: Thanks. I guess.

LEEANN: No problem. You know, Lily?

LILY: Yeah?

LEEANN: I know we've been mortal enemies since I stole your boyfriend.

LILY: Two boyfriends.

LEEANN: Two boyfriends? Oh...right. Well. I'm sorry. That was wrong of me. And I just want to say, I don't know, you should really let your friends know about your condition. So we can take care of you if you need help. I mean, you scared me to death.

KATARINA: You're lucky Simone was here.

MORGAN: She's totally going to make the headlines.

SQUID: I can see it now: Resident Nihilist Saves Life.

MIA: What's that all about, Miss Life Sucks And Then You Die?

SIMONE: What. I'm a hypocrite. So sue me. *(To Lily:)* Can I have my CD player back now?

LILY: Yeah. Thanks.

SIMONE: Just ask next time.

LILY: No. I mean. Thanks.

SIMONE: Don't mention it. Just remember to take your insulin.

LILY: I know.

SIMONE: No, really. Remember to take your insulin. You don't know what it's like to look at someone about to die. My brother did this to me once. I came home one day and he was napping. I just thought he was tired from school. But then a few hours passed and I got worried. I tried to wake him up but he wouldn't wake up. All he could do was stare at me. So I got his glucose set. I didn't even know what I was doing, my hands were shaking so bad when I was setting up the needle. But I did it. I gave him the shot because if I didn't—well, because I had to. And when he woke up, oh man, I yelled at him so bad.

LILY: I know. Normally I do. Three shots a day since I was nine. I'm not complaining. Most of the time it's no big deal. It's just a fact of life. Like flossing your teeth. But sometimes...you just don't want to do it. And when your dentist asks you if you've been flossing every day, you say, "yeah," and he looks at your bleeding gums and knows you're lying. Same thing. Sometimes you get this craving for a dozen sour cream Krispy Kremes straight out of the fryer. But you just took your injection and if you had that much sugar— well, you just say you're not hungry. Or this guy, who doesn't totally nauseate you, in fact, he kind of makes you laugh, finally invites you to check out his band after school. You are so dying to go, your stomach is tied up in knots. But you know that you just used your last bottle of insulin, so you tell him "maybe some other time" even though you know he'll never ask again. Sometimes you just want to break the rules because you're only seventeen once. You know it's not good for you, you know you shouldn't do it, but it shouldn't kill you.

(Everyone's quiet for a moment. Suddenly a cell phone rings. Everyone with a cell phone runs to check if it's theirs. There's obvious excitement. Could this nightmare be over?)

JEREMY: Yes.

KATARINA: Finally.

ROSIE: Oh, thank God.

LEEANN: That better be Bobby.

(It's Rosie's phone; she answers it.)

ROSIE: Hello?

MIA: Who is it?

DARCY: Shhh!

ROSIE: Mami? Ay Dios, I'm so glad to hear your voice. We're locked in the school library and this girl just had an insulin attack and the bathroom was locked and we don't have any more food and I like miss you so much—

VINCE: What's going on out there?

ROSIE: Shh! Hello? Mami? MAMI? Damn it, the signal cut out.

GARRETT: Are they coming to save us, or what?

(Rosie tries to call out. Nothing.)

ROSIE: Oh man, I hate these stupid things.

MORGAN: Did she say anything?

ROSIE: Yeah. She said...if I don't get home this second she's cutting off my long distance.

(*Rosie's tough exterior evaporates fast.*)

And I am like missing her so much right this second. I mean, I'm always all complaining about her and wishing an early painful death on her but she is like a truly amazing, kickass, take-no-prisoners kind of broad, you know? And she cooks a rice and beans that brings tears to your eyes it's so damn good. I'm always on her about starting a restaurant or something. I know we live in mini-mall land but I tell her these people have got to be hungry for some soul food, right? Anyway, that's my Mami and I have no idea why I'm going on about her.

LILY: Hey. Even I'm missing my parents. Don't worry about it.

(*Suddenly all the locks UNLOCK. The doors, the windows, the drawers, the vents. The lockdown is over.*)

MIA: What the hell was that?

SQUID: Someone check the door!

PIGEON: Got it. (*Trying the door:*) It's open.

(*Everyone cheers. An awkward silence.*)

What are we supposed to do now?

SIMONE: I guess we leave.

MIA: You'd think that someone would say something about something.

GARRETT: It's over. That's all I care about.

MORGAN: But that's just it. What's over?

LEX: I still think it was a malfunction.

DARCY: I'm sure Principal Walters will explain everything tomorrow morning during announcements.

ROSIE: No way, no how am I coming to school tomorrow.

LEEANN: So how come no one's leaving?

VINCE: Well...what about the noise?

GARRETT: Oh, dude, what if there's a dead body out there?

DARCY: Jeremy was right, though. If it was a shooting, there would have been sirens and police all over the place.

MIA: What if there's something wrong with the police?

KATARINA: That doesn't sound likely.

LILY: But so many things that didn't sound likely have been happening.

ROSIE: The girl's right. It's been pretty messed up lately.

ALICE: This is the worst part.

JEREMY: What's that?

ALICE: When the silence is on the outside and the noise is in your head. When you don't know the parameters, your brain overcompensates. Slowly the barometer of the possible gets re-calibrated and the most horrific things seem possible.

SQUID: I don't care what's out there. I'm not staying in here. *(To the cameras:)* You're gonna have to find another guinea pig. That's right. We've got our eyes on you! *(To Morgan:)* Hey, uh, you want a ride?

MORGAN: That'd be great. Oh, this is so *Sound of Music* when all the kids have to go to bed at that big party and they sing their song and each one has a different line.

SQUID: I'm glad to go...I cannot tell a lie.

MORGAN: I flit, I float. I fleetly flee, I fly.

(People can't help but sing the refrain. Morgan and Squid hit the road.)

ROSIE: Yeah. I don't care either. I'm out of here.

GARRETT: Hey, wait up. I'll give you a lift.

ROSIE: One move and I swear the karate comes out and smacks you in the face.

(Rosie walks out, Garrett spritzes his mouth with breath freshener and follows.)

LEX: He recovers fast.

MIA: I should get going too. Before my parents call in the National Guard. Anyone need a ride?

SIMONE: I do. You know, if you can stand me for another twenty minutes.

MIA: I think I can handle it. Hey. Can I—

(Simone hands No Exit over to Mia.)

SIMONE: You're going to love it.

(Simone and Mia leave. Lily tries to stand up.)

LILY: Whoa.

LEEANN: Careful.

LILY: I'm fine.

LEEANN: You may be fine but I'm driving you home and I don't want to hear any complaints because I can be a real bitch when I want to be and I think you've known me long enough to know that.

LILY: I think that's the sweetest thing I've heard all day.

LEX: What about you, Pigeon—I mean, Sophie? You need a ride?

KATARINA: Not that it's any of my business. But why are you called Pigeon, anyway?

PIGEON: I don't know. I don't really like pigeons. I mean, I don't dislike them. But they're not my favorite bird. I'm not saying anything against them. They've got their strong points. They're very smart and trainable and very loyal.

LILY: It was the day of the duck.

KATARINA: What?

LILY: Pigeon. Sophie was walking to school and there was this duck following her. And you know, by the time she got to school—

KATARINA: She's called Pigeon. Ah, high school. Well, by the time you're my age, you won't even remember the trauma any more. You'll actually start thinking: hey, maybe I should go to that tenth reunion. See what all those crazy people are up to.

LEX: No way. In seventy-one days I'm walking out that door, and I'm never looking back.

PIGEON: *(To her frogs:)* We're going home, guys.

(Lily, Leeann, Lex, and Pigeon leave. Darcy has taken down all her posters.)

DARCY: Guess I'm off.

KATARINA: Don't tell me the prom's been cancelled.

DARCY: Never—the prom must go on! But...I've been doing some thinking. I believe it is my duty as an elected official to start asking some hard questions of our administration. As such, I have developed a whole new postering concept. It's going to wake people up. It's going to make people think about what's happening in our school and why. Because I think there are some things that we need answers to.

KATARINA: Sounds like a guerrilla artist in the making.

DARCY: Yes...I think I like the sound of that.

(Darcy leaves.)

JEREMY: *(To Vince:)* I don't know about you, but I think I need some unwinding. What do you say we go kick some hobgoblin ass?

VINCE: Your house or mine?

JEREMY: Your mom's cooking is better.

VINCE: True.

(As they reach the door, Vince tenses.)

You really think it's safe out there?

JEREMY: I'll go first.

(They leave. Alice packs up all her books — it's got to be fifty pounds at least.)

KATARINA: Well, I guess the nightmare is over.

ALICE: So what are you going to go to school for?

KATARINA: What?

ALICE: Grad school. That's where you're going, right?

KATARINA: Yeah. Playwriting. I'm a playwright.

ALICE: Really? I'm into writing too. Any advice?

KATARINA: Yeah. Be a plumber.

(Katarina and Alice turn off the lights and leave. As the door bangs shut, the intercom clicks on.)

PRINCIPAL'S VOICE: Everything is fine. I repeat, everything is fine.

(The Sound of Music. Blackout. End of play.)

The Author Speaks

What inspired you to write this play?
I was commissioned by South Coast Repertory of Costa Mesa, CA to write a play for their Teen Players acting troupe. I then met the 11 girls and 4 boys who were in the troupe and asked them: what do you want in a play? And (perhaps just as importantly) what do you NOT want in a play? I heard about their acting experiences good and bad, their favorite and least favorite roles. The take-away for me was that they were all desiring characters they could relate to—people they see around their own school. I was inspired by the actors I met and my goal was to give each of them a real and substantial role in the play.

Was the structure of the play influenced by any other work?
Not particularly. But I do love plays that exist in real time and space. While there are time lapses between the scenes in *Lockdown*, I hope to create the sensation of the characters' long ordeal and the emotional strain of it. Waiting in a state of disinformation can be painful. The audience should feel the stress of this intense journey.

Have you dealt with the same theme in other works that you have written?
I often deal with the issue of feeling like an outsider. I suppose a writer often feels like an outsider—looking in, observing. I like to delve into the rawness of an emotion so that a character isn't simply saying "I'm scared" but allowing the audience to *feel* his or her fear. Then the audience is along on the journey—to experience the struggle and hopefully some form of triumph. I like an uplifting ending—but I don't like to answer all the questions. Will the kids go back to calling Sofie "Pigeon" tomorrow? Will new friendships be

formed or was this just a fluke?   This is the fodder for discussion.

What do you hope to achieve with this work?
Thematically, the play tackles some difficult topics — being different, feeling isolated, anger, intolerance, fear.   My goal is to tackle issues straight on and to create a sense of realness that sparks a conversation.   I hope that audiences see themselves and their peers in these characters, can relate, and can understand that they are, in fact, not alone.

To me, the play is only the first part of a production.   The second part is the discussion that grows out of the play.   Has anyone been made fun of by a best friend?   Have you ever called someone a nickname that they hate?   How do we treat people who are perceived as "different"?   What drives people to a cracking point?

This is not a play about a school shooting but there is a strange noise that could have been a gunshot and imaginations go wild.   I incorporated this to open the discussion up about what could drive someone to the point of fatal violence and what we can all do to make sure it doesn't happen.   What we can do lies in the very small decisions and interactions that happen all day everyday.   When we call someone "Pigeon" who doesn't want to be called Pigeon, what are we complicit with?

What are the most common mistakes that occur in productions of your work?
My plays move.   The rhythm of the language maintains a quick pace.   Except when it doesn't.   I love the sense of juxtaposition this creates.   For example, the peer repartee should zing like friends are quipping back and forth.   Then, when Alice takes the stage for her page-long monologue, the pace can slow down and the audience can be swallowed by

the images. Pick up your cues and don't let the pacing lag!

What inspired you to become a playwright?
I started writing plays before I knew what playwriting was.
When I was six, I have a distinct memory of putting on skits
with an older cousin. I recited AA Milne's poem, "Now I Am
Six" — and each year after that I tacked on a new verse. We
made our families buy tickets and watch us act and read
poetry. I have always been drawn to stories and I suppose I
understood early the power of live performance. As great as
TV and movies are, there's nothing quite like the visceral
energy live actors and live audience can create and experience.

**Shakespeare gave advice to the players in *Hamlet*; if
you could give advice to your cast what would it be?**
Each play I write has a heart. It's the idea or scene or
monologue that inspires the rest of the play — around
which I write the whole play. Each character also has a
heart — and it's the actor's job to figure out what makes
that character tick and to make it real. Sure you need to
learn your lines and your blocking. But you need to
know the *why* of your character. The more raw feeling
that you can imbue your character with, the more
emotionally involved the audience will feel. Good luck.
And have fun!

**How was the first production different from the vision that
you created in your mind?**
If I was a micromanaging playwright, I might have extensive
stage directions and line readings for the actors. Instead, I like
to create problems for designers, directors, and actors to solve.
It's the fun part of a collaboration. I also like to add some
whimsy into the mix. So when I say it's the CliffNotes Library

and the time is "Soon?" I am eager to see the solutions that the whole team devises. My play is a blueprint. The collaboration creates the vision.

About the Author

Julia Edwards is an LA-based playwright, children's author and illustrator, and teacher. Her plays—some of which include *Family Planning, The Rats Are Getting Bigger, The Ravaging,* and *Lockdown*—have been seen at The Public Theatre (NYC), the LAByrinth Theatre (NYC), The Flea (NYC), South Coast Repertory Theatre (Costa Mesa), Chalk Repertory Company (LA), Circle X (LA), and Salvage Vanguard Theatre (Austin) among others. *Family Planning,* produced in LA-area residential homes, won the LA Ovation Award for Best Production. She is a member of the Playwrights Union of LA. Her website is www.JuliaEdwards.com.

About YouthPLAYS

YouthPLAYS (www.youthplays.com) is a publisher of award-winning professional dramatists and talented new discoveries, each with an original theatrical voice, and all dedicated to expanding the vocabulary of theatre for young actors and audiences. On our website you'll find one-act and full-length plays and musicals for teen and pre-teen (and even college) actors, as well as duets and monologues for competition. Many of our authors' works have been widely produced at high schools and middle schools, youth theatres and other TYA companies, both amateur and professional, as well as at elementary schools, camps, churches and other institutions serving young audiences and/or actors worldwide. Most are intended for performance by young people, while some are intended for adult actors performing for young audiences.

YouthPLAYS was co-founded by professional playwrights Jonathan Dorf and Ed Shockley. It began merely as an additional outlet to market their own works, which included a substantial body of award-winning published and unpublished plays and musicals. Those interested in their published plays were directed to the respective publishers' websites, and unpublished plays were made available in electronic form. But when they saw the desperate need for material for young actors and audiences—coupled with their experience that numerous quality plays for young people weren't finding a home—they made the decision to represent the work of other playwrights as well. Dozens and dozens of authors are now members of the YouthPLAYS family, with scripts available both electronically and in traditional acting editions. We continue to grow as we look for exciting and challenging plays and musicals for young actors and audiences.

About ProduceaPlay.com

Let's put up a play! Great idea! But producing a play takes time, energy and knowledge. While finding the necessary time and energy is up to you, ProduceaPlay.com is a website designed to assist you with that third element: knowledge.

Created by YouthPLAYS' co-founders, Jonathan Dorf and Ed Shockley, ProduceaPlay.com serves as a resource for producers at all levels as it addresses the many facets of production. As Dorf and Shockley speak from their years of experience (as playwrights, producers, directors and more), they are joined by a group of award-winning theatre professionals and experienced teachers from the world of academic theatre, all making their expertise available for free in the hope of helping this and future generations of producers, whether it's at the school or university level, or in community or professional theatres.

The site is organized into a series of major topics, each of which has its own page that delves into the subject in detail, offering suggestions and links for further information. For example, Publicity covers everything from Publicizing Auditions to How to Use Social Media to Posters to whether it's worth hiring a publicist. Casting details Where to Find the Actors, How to Evaluate a Resume, Callbacks and even Dealing with Problem Actors. You'll find guidance on your Production Timeline, The Theater Space, Picking a Play, Budget, Contracts, Rehearsing the Play, The Program, House Management, Backstage, and many other important subjects.

The site is constantly under construction, so visit often for the latest insights on play producing, and let it help make your play production dreams a reality.

More from YouthPLAYS

Harry's Hotter at Twilight by Jonathan Dorf
Comedy. 90-100 minutes. 5-25+ males, 7-25+ females (12-50+ performers possible).

In this crazed mash-up parody of *Harry Potter* and *Twilight*—with cameos crashing in from *Lord of the Rings*, *Star Wars*, *Alice in Wonderland* and many other places—you'll encounter deli-owning vegetarians, invisible rabbits, magical carrot weapons, random lunatics, soothing offstage voices, evil gourmets and much more, as everyone's favorite wizards, vampires and werewolves battle to save miserable, gloomy Spork—and indeed the world—from certain destruction.

Techies by Don Goodrum
Comedy. 25-35 minutes. 5-6 males, 3-4 females (8-9 performers possible).

Overachieving high school senior Tony Sullivan just wants to get through one more production so that he can move on to Harvard and the rest of his life. But with overdramatic actors, overmedicated teachers and overprotective parents seemingly aligning to thwart his every move, will the show go on? Will Tony? A comic look at one of life's most important transitions and a loving tribute to the unsung heroes of the stage, the kids who sit in the dark and make the magic happen.

Twinkle Toes by Bradley Hayward
Dramedy. 30-35 minutes. 3 males, 3 females.

Calvin, a flamboyant high school senior, prepares for the most important day of his life. As his audition for the Julliard School of Dance approaches, he spends day and night on the dance floor. His friends and family rally at his side, but he has a broken heart that must be mended before he can stand on tiptoe and take his place in the spotlight.

Love (Awkwardly) by John Rotondo & Maryann Carolan
Comedy. 35-40 minutes. 4 males, 4 females, 3-6 either (8-14 performers possible).

Eddie is hopelessly in love with his best friend, Wendy, who is infatuated with another guy. Luke and Roxanne seem to have the perfect relationship. But she's about to graduate and go to Fordham, leaving him behind. Randy cheating on Charlotte with her best friend Laura. Last year, Laura broke up with George, Randy's close friend. George hasn't ever really recovered and still hopes desperately that she will come back to him. In its own comic fashion, ***Love (Awkwardly)*** follows these eight juniors and seniors through wonderful, painful, exhilarating moments and emotions that are adult in magnitude but cramped by the confines of high school. Also available in a full-length version.

Masks by Paul E. Doniger
Comedy. 100-120 minutes. 5 males, 6 females, 2 either and 6-12+ extras (19-40 performers possible).

A poignant and hilarious love story set in a struggling Commedia troupe. Young Pierette replaces her father in the comic performances, then nearly destroys the company by falling in love with the faithless Flavio. The mix of classic dell'Arte performances and the dramatic lives of the offstage actors creates a completely unique theatrical experience with challenging roles for all of the performers.

Of Love and Shampoo by Jonathan Josephson
Comedy. 30-35 minutes. 2 males, 2 females.

Life is pretty awful when you've accidentally locked yourself in the bathroom, especially on the night you're supposed to meet your girlfriend's parents. A madcap comedy about four friends, one very important date, and the locked door that brings them together.

Slow by Keegon Schuett
Drama. 45-55 minutes. 1 male, 3 females, 1 either.

Lizzy Slominski is better known to her classmates as "Camera Girl," because she's always hiding behind her digital camera snapping photos of strangers. Her days as a loner end when a mysterious new boy appears at the bus stop. Will she be able to put down her camera and connect, or is she doomed to a life of observing through the lens?

Multicultural Education by Alan Haehnel
Dark Comedy. 25-35 minutes. 2-18 males, 6-22 females (18-30 performers possible).

The day of the annual multicultural food fair starts normally enough for Ellen and her classmates at North Valley High. But each passing moment brings new and increasingly strange revelations—Sam arrives with grubs as his contribution to the fair; Lynda and Carmen's teacher forces them to wear head-to-toe coverings or be beaten; vigilante mobs attack students for not surrendering their food. By the end of the play, these typical high school students learn, quickly and drastically, that what they take for granted as Americans does not necessarily apply throughout the world.

Persephone Underground by Carol S. Lashof
Drama. 45-60 minutes. 2-15 males, 7-20+ females, 8-10 either (19-45 performers possible).

What do you do if your daughter runs away with the boyfriend from hell? Literally. If you're Demeter, the goddess of the harvest, you hold the entire earth hostage until her return. When eerie otherworldly music coming from a cave lures Persephone to seek the source, she meets a mysterious young demigod who proves to be the nameless son of Hades and follows him into the underworld. **Romeo and Juliet** and **Twilight** have nothing on this saga of unlikely lovers torn from Greek mythology.

Need

- computers/laptops ✓
- cell phones
- "A.T.U." + speakers
- Vents
- Book shelves (Painted on set?)
- Posters
- Clock (crystal - changeable by tech crew)
- food items (scene 4)
- ~~SAT~~ Prep book

---

backpack
Syringe

Posters
Pe SEOS
cell phones

Made in the USA
Charleston, SC
15 July 2015